Serenade

x

Saudade

MAJDA ULFAT

AURAQ

Printed in the Islamic Republic of Pakistan.
Printed: November, 2020
Edition: 1st
ISBN: 978-969-749-042-4
Price: Rs 900 PKR, $09 US

ISLAMABAD, PAKISTAN

raabta@auraqpublications.com | +92-300-0571-530
www.auraqpublications.com | @AuraqPublications
ISBN : 978-969-749-042-4

Contents

Serenade

I serenade myself with

lullaby of imagination

to confront the reality

All vibes are welcomed here

no matter what kind of vibes they are

the moment I embrace them completely

they don't become good vibes

but they become something beyond it

that moment it becomes a mirror

reflecting me my strength my weakness all of me whispering
to me

that I am

self-sufficient and I can do it.

This world is still beautiful, all thanks to dreamers and their dreams.

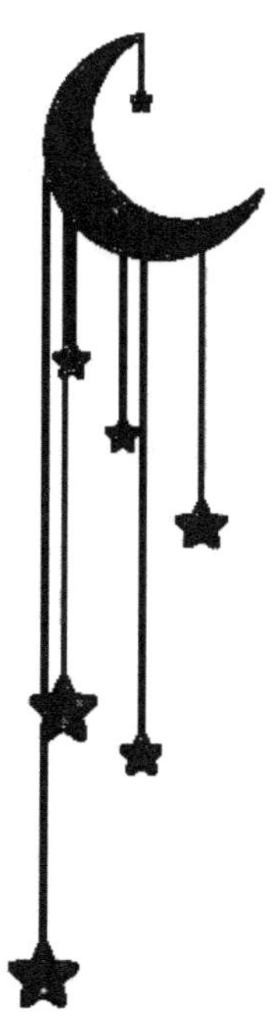

Life has imprisoned us in the prison called reality thank goodness dreams provide the key to break it.

Protect your dream, they are too precious to be left at the mercy of reality.

Dreams that you have dreamt

with your opened eyes

are the most beautiful thing

You have come so far

you can't give up now

The path you used to tread upon

are now paths

you must continue

its better to have sleepless eyes

than to have dreamless eyes

When dark shadows hover over my heart

when the demons scream loudly

I seek refuge by dreaming..

I am convinced that

dreams are not foolery

it is a luxury and of course

dreamers are the richest..

I changed a lot of things

what I couldn't change was reality

and what reality couldn't change was my heart

I am still at war with reality

standing at the arsenal of hope

wearing the armour of fantasy.

If I can't be the star

that shines for eternity

then let me be the cloud

that comes in dawn

grows in morning

glows in noon

calls upon the other clouds

through the day

makes the wind pleasant

in the afternoon ,glitters with setting sun

in the horizon

dazzles with silver outline.

in the evening

delights everyone

with thunder and rain

and then disappears...

I am also like you

a helpless,

a beautiful dreamer,

a firefly lost in darkness

I too have dreamt of blossom in frost.

I can feel the taste of words a lot subtle and sweet

all the paths doubtful and blurred

will be crystal clear now

through the dark sky

through thick clouds I'll fly

everything that comes my way is good

even if I fall I know

I can get right up again

They can stop pitying

and start being in awe all the dreams I see

are full of glee

seems like they renewed my eyes.

I can see everything once I start dreaming

Sometimes insanity imparts us with greater sanity. Insanity regarding dreams, ideas and goals are the most sanest insanities.

Behind the smiling face

I know your heart is out of place

I don't have words enough to solace

But soon spring will melt this glace

No matter how much paths bend

Remember it's not the end

Towards you I will endlessly extend

My hand, you aren't alone, my friend

Throughout the day

I only pray

"Bridges that you've burnt may

Light up your way"

When nothing seems bright

In your every sleepless night

In your hour of plight

I wish to be your light.

I am here, don't try

to hide when you cry

even if your tears don't dry

on me you can always rely

So in this darkest hour

stay strong, don't cower

soon in happiness you will shower

soon spring will come to you too,

my flower.....

Soon there'll be dawn with morning dew

it'll be a day bright and new

with courage just pull through

you are not alone I stand by you

You can't see stars and moonlight

tears cloud your sight

just breathe and smile through this night

everything will be alright

I know it was another troublesome day

but it wont forever stay

You will surely find your way

Everything will be okay

Tainted memories that whole day you fight

comes as nightmare at night

but listen hold on tight

dont cower in fright you can't your despair conceal

I think I know how you feel

That isn't your life a hamster wheel

Your tears fall and you keel

Just forget yesterday, seize the present

Don't worry about tomorrow enjoy the present

Try to stop the feeling of repent

Smile and send away your every lament

We have tread upon countless places

only in the wish to find a place to stand

We have met thousands of faces

only in the wish to a find those who can understand.

We humans, after losing way on an unknown road

stumble and cry like a lost child

asking for help from strangers

trying to find a way back home

but like a lost child

we also don't know where's our home.

If I can find myself and look at myself

Then its never too dark for me.

Dazed

Is it getting dark or is it getting bright

is it dawn or evening

was I like this from the start

am I chasing my dream

or am I being chased by nightmare

why am I tired when I didn't do anything

why am I saying I am fine

when I found myself tear drenched again

why did I laugh so hard

when I didn't feel like even smiling

am I really living or just breathing

where am I ?

Who is writing this?

Is it you or is it me?

It seems like forever I am wandering around

the same place the same ground

my footsteps feel tired now

I don't know how

to continue

perhaps all but few

find the road

I am just carrying this haggard soul's load

the haunting consequences that I fear

are already here

that in search of a way

my own self is drifting away

in this journey I have lost

myself, this is the cost

I am afraid
that I have paid.

The path I had been striding on

is what I considered a paragon

in the dark a diamond that shone

Alas now its lustre all gone...

We are bound to follow different future

here ends my little venture

your thoughts were a sweet quencher

o dear path !!!remember my forlorn adventure

Tis the end of harsh fantasy

A mere foolery which I called consistency

yet you interpreted as incompetency

tis a total times fallacy...

Do you know in search of your trace

how many tears did I embrace?

now I want a new path to face

I want to tread to a different place

I want to hear unheard melody

I have taken a step back from you already

I am escaping your threnody

thinking at some point I will find a remedy

in front of me winding paths came

that changed the directions are the one to blame

yet my destiny is still the same

I tend to walk on my altered paths with this sole aim...

The familiar darkness continues to prevail

With each breath that I helplessly inhale

All the tears and painful the wail

Despite struggles why do I always fail?

Dear destiny answer me! Where are you?

Don't you know how much did I tread to pursue?

the forbidden forgotten dreams of you that became forlorn longings but did not come true

Like that road with endless folds

Like moonlight that hide behind the cold clouds

Faded away are all the footholds.

I don't know anymore what this vague future holds

Dear destiny please reach out so heavy are the burdens I schlep.

please let me hear your footstep.

knowing that you are close I will take every step

towards me just take the single one step...

Walking beside the time's rivulet.

I wonder where these paths end Perhaps to an acquaintance

I've before met.

Or into the dark wood ahead.

I don't know what is beyond my sight yet.

May be it leads to a flower field.

Or to the destiny of goals that I've set Perchance to the place

where I can my thoughts fend.

Or to the laments where I might down let.

Mayhap to the mistakes which now I might mend

All the paths I must carefully vet.

But I ought to follow them wherever they send.

With struggle to find the path I wish to get...

Apparently I am ready to face any trial

determined to walk thousand a mile

with my big bright smile

believing that every struggle is worthwhile

but the lips which say the line

I am alright I am fine

the eyes that so brightly shine

they are not mine

Because there's a mask I wear

hiding all my despair

concealing every nightmare

pretending as if walking on air

When it wears

out, I put more layers

beneath which I am falling apart but who cares

Probably in this world we all are mere players

Beneath this adorned mask

real me helplessly ask

the providence of impossible task

why there's no glory to bask

Through the mask no one can see

the real me the melancholic me

the one left with no glee

the real me the crying me

I yearn for a day when all pains depart

when happiness finds this foolish heart

then this mask will fall apart

ending its never-ending art...

Dear sorrow!!!!

can't you come tomorrow

instead, let me borrow

a peaceful moment ,some time

let the things be sweet as nursery rhyme

for a while let my demons sleep

today I don't want to weep

nor do I want to think too deep

I want to rest

don't put my heart to the test

for once let me indulge in laughter

so come not today, come the day after....

It is really fine to take

some chance to make some mistake

in my sorrows scars there's a grace

I want to fully embrace

myself without trying to hide

in my worn out yet stubborn self I take pride

I no longer wish to be understood

I stand tall n lone but now I am all good now nothing more I

ask for

go ahead and abhor

I am not a difficult book so stop that frown

perhaps others like reading upside down

I have my destiny to follow
in whatever they say I no more wallow

Even if sorrows eat

me, even if defeat

surround me

Lets not retreat

Even if my tears wash away

all my courage, even if we lose our way

lets not stray...

Within my sorrow when I sink

when I don't find anyone to sync

I am forced to think

whenever I am at brink

why all the people I trust disappear in a blink

to console I turn my tears into ink

and all the words and rhymes I link

constitutes something called poem...

I'm your thought from yesterday

your forgotten words

your forlorn wish

your abandoned dream

do you remember how long you had thought of me

writing my name in your secret notes

dont you remember the cold winter eve I came to you

perhaps you dont remember anything

is it my fault that you've come across

so many hurtful gloomy thoughts

that you forgot me

I don't wish for you to remember me, next time if you ever

come across me

read me with a familiar face

read me with acquaint grace...

Of all the people

who have turned stranger

the most unfamiliar stranger

to me was myself

In search of people

in order to bring those strangers back

I had long forgotten the real me

its being me who estranged myself...

Why do you blame others ,always looking those who came not for your rescue why always burning in flames of being ignored why do you need to be left on mercy of others. Stand up! you are a hero of your own. Get up you are saviour of your own

not a mere survivor. Even you have been oblivious of yourself, when you stumble and fall why you always look around to see who laughed and who saw? Why don't you see if you are hurt or not? I only hope next time you fall. Tightly EMBRACE YOURSELF who has been hurt. LOVE YOURSELF who has withstood greater pain. Be HAPPY to be someone this strong,

be PROUD to stand up after falling....

You must've been to the sea but have you ever rode the waves ,more importantly have you ever been caught up in a whirlpool where there's nothing to hold onto all you can do is to wait until its over if you haven't then don't think everyone has been through something similar what you've seen is the just the beautiful blue surface of it what someone else have seen could be the atrocious dark depths of it therefore don't invalidate others feelings and emotions...

Things like miracles

things like winter flowers

and the spring snow are the

sweetest.

If you can't see your wings

fault lies in the way you see

things not in your wings.

Our thoughts are the freest

Yet they hold us slaves.

Our greatest strength lies our smiles

in our age it is no more expression of happiness

but expression of strength

stay strong!!!!

Kindness doesn't hurt little courteous act of kindness does make a difference. It doesn't hurt if you listen to same story twice or even thrice. It doesn't hurt if you laugh of unlaughable joke rather than saying its not funny .It doesn't hurt if you eat slightly salty food rather. Trust it won't hurt still you feel that something is hurting inside you its probably ego but hurting your ego is better than hurting others.

Writing isn't always bleeding

it's about healing yourself and others.

It feels again your luck overslept

all the tears that you've wept

all the pain to yourself that you've kept

has all got swept

That ugly looking evil induced fall

failure that's what you call?

Is it really everything? Is it really all?

it doesn't make you weak or small

- 62 -

Does it really matter?

when the dream is bigger better that doesn't shatter

when the hope doesn't scatter

Failure is not everything

actually its nothing

compared to the flowers of spring and everyday the gifts

and miracle life continues to bring.

When you come across

such petty worldly loss

you'll see there's hidden gloss

beneath every loss...

Only reason you fell down

is that you can rise again

a little brighter

a little higher..

The days have gotten again so long

I wonder where have I went so wrong

with life its hard to get along

such thoughts continue to throng

through every dark day

through all the doubtful noises

I will make my way

hearing that clear voice

You might see me fall

teary might get my eyes

but that's not all

get ready to see me rise

now matter how hard it has been

once again I begin

I can never give in

it isn't over until I win

They are trying to define

to confine

me, blaming that fault is all mine

to me its not fine

their rules, ugh an evil design

for me its a sign

to break the line

to take them down

no matter how much they frown

I can no more act like their clown

even if they're best in town

no matter how much they groan

I've got to overthrow their so called throne

tis time to cut what they've sown

They tried to shake me from the core

their audacity is real eye sore

but the struggle and pain I bore

couldn't tore

me apart, it built me stronger than before

for now I'll cry less and sweat more

then for them to escape there's no door

my tears will become their heavy rains

for them only regret remains

I'll break the chains

I'll end all the pains

It doesn't matter how frequently

you fall down what matters

is how often you get up from

that fall..

Falling down could be

a miracle

if you end up

finding yourself...

What is it? that light? Piercing and splendid?

Glowing jewel or fallen star that shimmers its shower.

An absolute beauty which will never be ended.

As I approach, tis a lake of flowers.

Ruling entire field, sparkling whole territory.

The flower's sun, the sunflower.

 Secretly heeding its story.

Listening carefully as it says.

A tale hidden behind its glory.

Although all the time the sun I chase Often realizing I can't
overcome these distances.

No matter what can't clear up this ever spreading haze.

At times envious of the planet that around it fences.

The pouring rain makes my spirit even drier.

Prevailing dusk at evening bring me trances.

Yet I am thankful to this mighty ball of fire.

For lighting up each place and every rift.

With your subtle warmth, I overcome times the dire

After hearing all, I began to drift.

But even now, through my heart that story continues to sift.

You are like a star always shining brightly

if you ever feel lonely

let me be your sky

so when' you want to shine

I would embrace all your darkness

and let you shine on night sky and if you ever want to hide

| will hide you

and I will shine on you warmly and brightly.

All I deserved were

the vague recollections of

nothing but my very own dreams.

So today I found a note in my abandoned notebook

 which made me cry and the note reads

"Always keep smiling'

The rain that appears

so clean and clear

its beautiful yet merciless

in the morning I have found

The young and green leaves

lying lifeless on the ground

while some old withered leaves

are still hanging in there

broken are the trees who used to stand tall

while still standing are the small

ones,

this rain is beautiful yet merciless

this fate is predestined yet ironic...

I am offended by that dark cloud that swallows the moon and intrigued by that moon that keeps defying the darkness of the cloud..

Everyone has some secret unrequited love for the

moon

though they aren't really looking

at the moon, they are actually

looking through the moon

to some far off place..

Another day ends

that's how in tomorrow today bends

at this time my heart no more pretends

with tears , it sends

off this day...my burdened soul is bereaved by your existence

You, who shine between today and tomorrow ,who brightens

the night ,to whom I tell all the weary stories all the heart

wrenching tales .Perhaps you know so much, you have seen

too much as well, I wonder if you will come down ever

and talk back too?

tell me too how lonely it is

to be surrounded by the stars!!!

tell me how it feels

to be surrounded by the dark ,perhaps you are afar

yet you always walk with me

guiding me through the dark

though you are always there

I might forget you when sun rises but I will instantly

search for you again

its not that I am obsessed or sleepless

I am not the Jupiter

I have only one moon

whether you're waning or rising

Demons have dug a deep swamp

and I have fallen deeply into it

Deep inside me I feel a lump

These feelings, I can't really dump

the higher I try to jump

the deeper I fall

it feels like a slump

These thoughts are like shackles

which continues to clump

me, but your voice gently spoke you aren't a poetry pump

its alright to stumble and stump

its okay to take the time

and forget the rhyme

take the time to recharge

strong you must stay

words will come your way

Poet knows no way of harm

inflict with him pain,

render him all wounded,

yet he won't complain

he would simply serenade you with a poem

Isn't it dangerously harmless???

Its amazing how much a muse

can inspire a person

You take the inspiration

And create something

Sometimes it goes beyond that

You are so inspired that your

Muse makes you want to live

And that moment you realise

That life is also an art

All thanks to muse...

My muse doesn't just inspire me to write.

It inspired me to be me

to keep going despite everything

not to run away

to make best use of my life

it taught me of how to be spring in winter

I am thankful the way you've

inspired me..

I have been writing for years

But when I found my muse

I started living..

An unfamiliar melody has just reached my ears

It somehow elegiac appears

out my heart wears

I can see how this sonata jeers

Of rout It sounds

In my empty heart it rebounds

And my heart helplessly pounds

It really astounds

Yet apart from these echoes, I can hear your voice

Crystal clear, pure as ice

Telling me believing in you is suffice

Shortly there will be time of rejoice

Although it hasn't been any gloat

but I won't wallow in this demote

because all I have to do is to devote

To give this symphony a harmonious ending note

Today recalling the near and distant past

I saw myself as I wouldn't even last

Gale was blowing everywhere so fast

Strange darkness it was about to cast

Times were also stern

I had nowhere to turn

Its okay cause of what I earn

Realizing I had so much to learn

I had my destiny there to seek

Although many of enemies reek

But I kept myself calm and meek

I became strong from what they thought as weak

Thinking back days of never ending mope

when there was still hope against hope

stumbled everywhere no place to lope

with those defeats I hardly cope

Today these memories are no big deal

that's how I really now feel

Every single wound found a heal

I walk upright I no more reel

Now as I stand

with strange fortitude in my hand

Everything is so clear and

many enigmas I have come to understand

 Regrets, having absolutely none

yet still having a last one

had so many regrets to across my mind run
this regret is my last one...

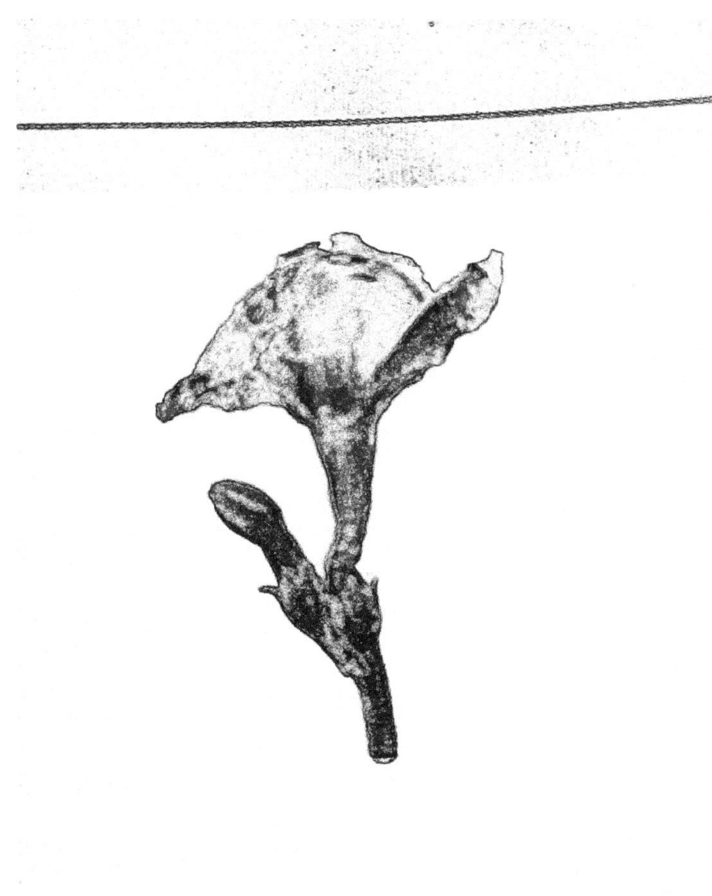

I had always thought that most beautiful flower is rose, even in my childhood whenever I looked at rose I would've lost in it for a minute. But it turned out I was wrong the most beautiful flower was the one my mother brought me in her way back from the walk. It was petite white flower overflowing with love I put it in my book but even now when I see it , it is so lovely and it is beautiful because it is filled with purest form of love, mother's love.

Existence of cats is a blessing to

humans. They'll make you laugh without you realizing and

make you

anticipate every moment

which would otherwise be monotonous. They are truly

magical.

When a loner feels lonely

that time It's awfully lonely...

What others consider prison they call it freedom .The darkness others fear they enjoy it and when someday tries to get close to them They push them away because they are enough for their own selves. Loners can't help thrashing loneliness upon them. They like submerging into it, it's comfortable this way for them, leaning on their own selves alone. Cushioning against their own thoughts...

$$x=?$$

- 99 -

Does darkness has a name?

yes sometimes it does it could be

misery ,loneliness, depression sadness ,

or even ourselves

does darkness has a name?

no sometimes it doesn't it could be anything sometimes its

nameless and hard to find too

hard to know the reasons behind it too

sometimes its just like **x.**

unknown and difficult to find sometimes its just

x.

$x=$ Love Bombing

Their sweets words are sugar coated poison

They don't actually mean it

they just want to burdened you

by their so called love

Their love smeared words are the womb of

the demons crawling in your head

To their words is connected

Invisible scaffold which has entangled you

Break away from it ,

run as fast as you can!!!!

Its not bad to run away for your life for your peace....

x=Gas Lighting

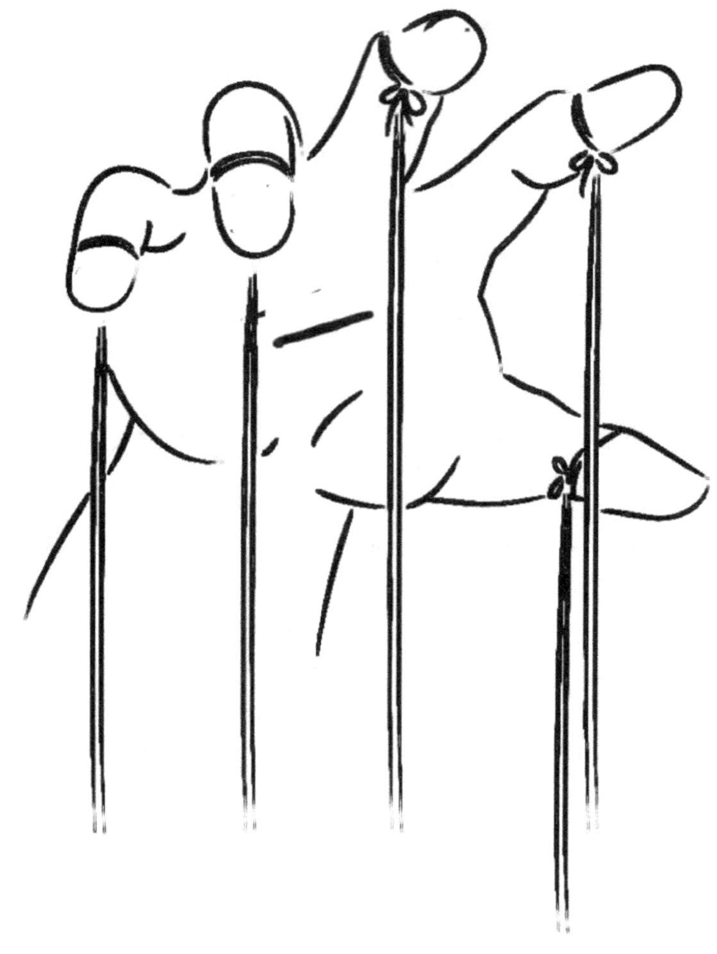

They say, you said that,

You are dramatic

you are outcast

here you go you are overreacting

everything is your fault

now hop on guilt train

they've just fuelled the engine

and driving it on expense of your sanity

and don't listen to their words

they inject with you thoughts that aren't yours

they made you their puppet following them

beware its power they seek

of toxic poison they reek

they wont let you speak

all the want is to make you weak...

break away from the thread tying you down

let them frown

stomp on their crown

find your real self again

free yourself from this pain....

x=Schizophrenia

Those voices became a shadow

those shadows became real

some were friends

playing fondly with lonely me

some were foes

haunting me each moment

some were flying angels

some were crawling demons

chasing me all the time

where should I seek refuge?

my turmoil is huge

but others say they dont see a thing

who should I turn to?

everyone is so perspective so stern to

strange me,

must I suffer for chemical imbalance of my brain?

Must I be held responsible for seesaw games

of dopamine and serotonin?

must I be ashamed of being different?

must I blame myself for things I don't control?

my faint self buried deep under the mound

of these demons answered," No,

You were sailing in dark you must seek

help from the light house

that light house is meant for you

it is meant for us"

x=Self Harm

The pain you can't show

your tears that continue to flow

was overflowing probably

you were fighting under sun

with no shade

then you grabbed the blade

to analgesize your greater

pains with a cut or few

these cuts looked as haven

to silence your demons

your blood inked lines

calmed the chaos in you for a while

these scars tattooed on your skin

tell the story which you couldn't tell

but I want to look beyond the scar

to the beautiful person behind it

dont be afraid or lonely

ashamed or worried

healing takes care and time

when the dark night will fade

you'll be no longer afraid

to throw away every blade

I'll welcome all the stories

hidden behind the scars

its alright,you aren't alone

I can listen it all

whenever you want to say

I'll be here

Of all the chances that you've been giving to others you deserve some of them yourself as well so give yourself a hug a cup of coffee lots of second chances and start over again..

Serenade X Saudade

You are writing a story

"of strength and endurance where

Everyday there is a battle

Every thought is a weapon

Every place is a battle field

And you are a hero

Standing alone, one moment wanting to be saved other

moment fighting by yourself

Continuing despite falling , despite injuries"

Keep writing your story please continue to write it I may sound desperate and I am desperate to keep reading that story, if not me there must be someone who wants to read it or even you read it yourself;

I hope and pray you let go of everything that bothers you,let go of everyone thats suffocating you just don't let go of yourself.

Keep writing your story take a break and continue again please do not put fullstop to it lets just put a semicolon to it;

I want to write a subtle reminder

to the one who is a warrior

today who is a survivor

and tomorrow who is gonna be a thriver

I am glad you exist

I am proud to see you resist

to that dark spreading mist

I believe your struggle wont go amiss

when I raise my hand and bring them together

I pray may every weather

you encounter blooms in spring

I pray with all my heart

even if my words cant reach you all

I continue to pray that may you overcome fall

your every feeling is valid

even if everyone invalidates them

your own self is worth living for

even if no body tell you

this world would definitely be dark without you

this world is beautiful with you in it

so I plead you to keep fighting;

Earlier today it rained heavily

I went down the street for a little strolling

I found some tiny petals of flower which

would've bloomed beautifully if

the rain had been little gentle were

scattered lifelessly flowing with rain water.

It reminded me of those beautiful souls

That would've been with us if we and the life had been little

gentle with them.

In the end blame is all on the

flower to be fragile but not on the rain to be harsh...In the

end blame is on them

to not have held on longer

But not on us who didn't hold them...

Wake up!

You'll be surprised by the miracles you can do.

Wake up!

You'll be surprised what tragedies you can prevent...

Wake up!

Little empathy doesn't hurt

Wake up!

Before they decide to sleep.

Wake up!

Extend your hand

and reach out to those who are walking in dark.

Wake up.

and show them their light

who are firefly lose in dark.

The thing about healing is you must not rush it, healing takes time. Everyone has different pace of it.

If you rush it, it has side effects therefore sometimes all you can do is to wait though it hurts, it hurts a lot but for healthy and proper healing you just give your wound some time.

People will tell you that to heal a wound ,you have to stop touching it but they wont tell you to take care of it to wash it .They won't tell you to do its dressing in most sterilized ways and to look at it often to check if its been healing well , to check if its not infected. They won't tell you that once it gets all healed up you have to tell others how much you have took care of it and you don't have to hide it under your sleeve.

- 120 -

You need to proudly tell others and thereby also tell them ways to avoid it or ways to heal it.

 Remember healing lies in owning your wound in cleaning it and in healing others.

I wish that these words

become a soft handkerchief and wipe away all your tears

all the sorrows and every grief

And these rhymes

become a warm embrace for you in these cold times

Majda Ulfat

Sit down for a while
it's okay you don't have to smile

Demons are crawling inside your head
I know you have to tread

On that dark lone road
to you, unknown is your abode

Probably it has been years
since you've been shedding tears

Yet neither can I console you
nor can I pat you

I'll be just walking nearer
holding in my hand a mirror

So that you can see your light
reflecting in it, ,all beautiful and bright

You are like a firefly lost in dark
unaware of your own spark

I don't wish to be your light
I just wish to show you your light

So get up now, let it reflect on you
let it shine on you...

There is a possibility things won't go the way you want, there is a possibility you would have to take professional help therapies and medications may be but its nothing to be ashamed of. Now imagine you're a knight but you need to use all the weapons present on your arsenal no doubt

 you are strong

 but

you must go beyond fist fight now grab the sword and

save yourself!!!

Saudade

There are some of those beautiful souls

who are your life

yet are not supposed to be in your life

but they house your heart entirely and,

light up your heart all the way to your soul,

they enlighten your whole life and brighten your eternity

God bless those beautiful souls.

"Saudade" is dedicated to those shining souls.

I wish you were here

If only you were here

neither would I have any fear

nor would I shed a tear

The winter wouldn't be so cold if only I could hold

your hand

Time keeps sifting through like the sand.

days pass, become months

then years

I am at same place

with never drying tears

and undying wish for you to be here

your thoughts ,your every flashback

has taken me a back

I wish you would come back
but alas, this is what reality has to lack.

I met a wanderer

on my way

who appeared to be tenderer

than the autumn's bright day

he was a passenger

of the same road

a stranger yet not a stranger

owing to whom, many paths I strode

A thousands miles

were lightened up

by his warm smiles

but sadly his journey was short

and our season faded away

It was a beautiful yet fleeting

A miracle, a mirage in the desert

that warm meeting..

Fog has spread up

right before my eyes

it keeps thickening

strangely reminds me of you

It doesn't disappear

I cant seem to avoid it

Neither can I escape it

Nor can I find it

its all around me

It keeps thickening more

it feels like

it would choke me

like your absence did

like your void like your thoughts

it keeps widening more

I can't see anything other than this

all the paths are invisible

feels like I have been blinded

I try to touch it but I can't

it's there but not there

just like you...

Probably it's fall

trees that used to stand tall

blooming and colourful all

have began to stall

no matter if it's fall or bloom

for me its always gloom

autumn after autumn

what's so special about spring

in the end it will bring

the fall again

what's the point of blooming so brightly

in the end it all will wither..

That rain

That taps your window pane

That is making the moon wane

That lightning and thunder

That makes you wonder

About me,,, is not so tender

That rain,, you are watching alone

Thinking of us in time flown,

Like the clouds separated by wind blown

Don't send it to me

Don't show it raindrops

because the raindrops are every flashback

Of us in rain in day and night black

I wish I could take few steps back

Perhaps these clouds are the reason why

My tidings couldn't reached the sky

Like flying clouds I had to away from you fly

This rain lone I'm watching owed

my eyes just rain and cloud

But no joy as it vowed

So in this long run

I'm better off with scorching sun

And with this solitary rain I'm done.

So wait shortly to you I will come somehow

To see with you all the rain and snow

And the enchanting rainbow

So don't send this solitary rain to me

Don't show this solitary rain to me....

Cold winter is drawing near

after a while it will be here

how will I bear

it, I fear..

It reminds of that cold

evening, that felt like a nightmare

can I be bold

enough to survive through that

despair?

I don't want winter to come.

oh summer can't you stay longer

I am afraid to become

overwhelmed by that nostalgic sadness

like the insects which gather

food to live through winter

I am trying to gather

all my courage to live through this winter

or spending it in a slumber

like those animals I want to sleep

so I can't remember

that agony and those tears to weep

It got me all numbed

the thought of that first snow

falling down like my tears

steady and slow

I wish for a change of sequence this time

I long for a spring before this frost

please spring find us this once

before I am permanently lost...

All around flowers are blooming

brightly

wind also seems so gentle today

yet my heart is all glum

still plunged in fall

I miss the time

when you were spring

and I was a mere flower

The blossom of dreams

that we dreamt still shine bright

Look spring has come again

but you haven't

Now that you aren't here

the spring

feels so autumn

its funny spring without you is still called spring

Even if you don't come back

I only pray that autumn

doesn't dare to bother you

With this spring wind

I send you the earnest of my tidings

that bloomiest of the spring reaches you..

When I heard that voice again

I was half smiling and half

tearing up

That was a compass

when I was wandering alone.

I miss that voice that won't answer my echoing cries now that voice that won't return but more than that voice I want to hear that breath that used to bear that voice...

There is no

bigger tragedy than

oblivion.

I found new things at the same old place

I guess it wasn't trust but oblivion

now you can name this oblivion as indifference

so that I can also stop being hero

and act as a pitiable villain

and punish myself with some pain

and with a lot of remorse

its strange how an insanely dark day

can make a hero a villain..

Now that I think of how

I found my spring

in your winter

Light ,in your darkness

A haven ,in shadows hovering around you and on top of

That

I mistook your smile

as your happiness

I was oblivious just as ever

I can see what an atrocious regret

and melancholy oblivion can bring

Sometimes we haven't done anything wrong

yet oblivion gets better of us and

takes us off guarded...

*The price of oblivion
is a lifetime filled with regret..*

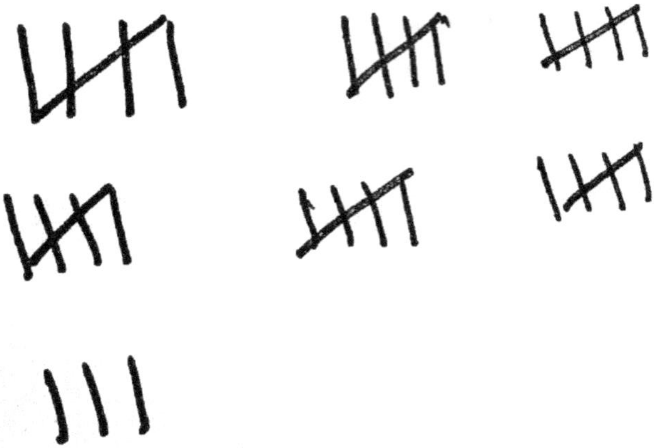

- 150 -

Tears can't hide behind any word

your sweet voice that I heard

flew away with you as an angel as a bird

how can I ever reword

you just went away

painting my world all grey

what can I say

about that darkest day

that cruellest coldest December

how can I not remember

it is difficult to clamber

through this December

You have gone asleep

giving me a hard promise to keep

saying don't cry don't weep

it's hard as my wound is so deep

tis time difficult to swallow

see you again dearest fellow

will hear your voice sweet the mellow

this goodbye is a promised hello

though my heart is scarred

I won't let down my guard

rest well you worked hard

goodbye my star you worked really hard

somehow I will live well

know that you did really well

tis grieving to tell

to bid you my farewell

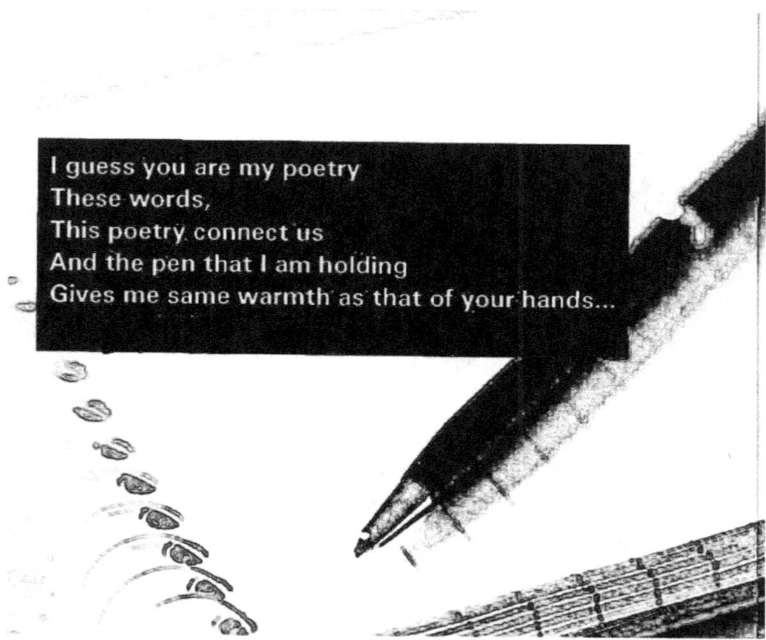
I guess you are my poetry
These words,
This poetry connect us
And the pen that I am holding
Gives me same warmth as that of your hands...

Same time ticking on the clock

no matter how they mock

I am still in shock

feels like my optimism hitting the bottom rock

I am gathering all my hopes to knock

at the door of miracle

to you, it may sound lyrical

but for me even breathing is obstacle

because I miss you

Out of longing and love I have for you

With the little flickering spark

I have, I will continue to walk

through the dark

I will continue to smile

through every trial...

We were such a warm dream

A bond stronger than a team

remember how we used to gleam

how beautiful we used to seem

The fact that you who shone

so brightly is gone

is a nightmare from which I can't move on

to this darkness there is no dawn

Now I am alone drenching in the rain

of memories, this pain

now in my mirthless poems remain

but those times can't comeback again

Even if you have left everything behind

you are always on my mind

soon I will come to find

you, once these paths unwind...

You are gone It's been awhile

I am still in denial

All the hopes are now probably futile

yet I still miss your smile

it beckons me to overcome every trial

I know you are in a better place

in these words its hard to find solace

I still miss your face

your absence has carved a place

deep in my heart resembling your silhouette

Now I am making memories

with your memories

stories

with your words

perhaps an attempt worth making

to widen a space which always

remain intact for us.

All of our time passed so fast

in front of goodbye I stand aghast

your void in me is still so vast

I am sorry an enthusiast

like me would leave you in past

I guess I would have to send you off at last

My heart is weary

but I won't call you a mere memory

through the times I will carry

you in my heart, oh my brightening sanctuary

I will continue to write your story

to show everyone your light your glory

In the dust of time I won't let you fade

I'll keep all the promises I made

I'll neither be swayed

nor be afraid

I will go to farthest future under your shade

Together with you like a shadow

to the distant future I will go

I'll send you off

but I will never let go of you

your smile

your memories

your dreams

even your tears

I don't want to forget any of it

you are far too precious

to let go of just because you aren't here....

Has the snow melted?
Has the spring come to you?
If it hasn't then let me
trade my springs with your falls
for me even your fall is spring...

Just like those petals.

that are on the same flower.

we were right next to each other like them fighting every shower and every drop of rain.

Fighting every scar and pain.

But alas it all went in vain.

As the time passed our intervening fate ended, by the winds of same ironic fate

we drifted away

we withered away

as if spring never even came our way....

You are not a mere memory

You are a story

Which constitutes all the

Pages of the notebook

Called my life.

Just go with burden less heart

I will hold the candle so you can

see your way

and I will hold my tears too

so the candle doesn't go out

just go without a regret and tears

leave all of it to me

and when we meet on the other side

just recognize me and remember that

I was always by your side...

My side has become empty with your absence but this empty side is not a misery because it serves as a reminiscent of your presence...

- 168 -

*How can that same breath-taking scenery look so plain just by **your***

absence

Sometimes providence of everything of all the happening are

just to remind me of you and

God be praised those are the sweetest

and most beautiful providences.

I don't necessarily miss you
at a certain day or certain time
or at a particular occasion .
when I miss you the interval
between seconds extend infinitely
and I find my eternity between
those seconds.

Meeting you was like reading a short but beautiful poem that ends soon but leaves an impact.

For the dearest friend

who I miss

the one faraway I had to send

Whose existence is a pure bliss

whose story continues to extend

as I continue with memories to reminisce

The rain of tears may pour

yet I smile thinking about you

Though I can see you no more

Yet I talk about you

As if you have just walked out of the door

I remember you

As brightest day just like before

Not keeping it as a promise nor a vow

Just thinking about you while I sit

Just like a favourite hobby

And old habit

thank you to the memories you endow

all the paths I take are lit...

- 173 -

Perhaps I am a disbeliever who doesn't believe you are gone

or may be I am a believer who believes you will comeback.

If fate has compassion then there will be miracle and if the miracle has compassion then there will be you again...

- 175 -

Just like the hope of spring denies the frost Like the hope of finding destiny keeps me going despite being lost the hope of meeting you again will keep me going through storm and rain through this parting grief and pain.

Now I'll simply withstand

wounds that wont heal

now I'll simply understand

that all questions won't find answers

I'll adorn your memories with poem

until we meet again

I'll survive every storm

and all the rain

Neither would I try to escape

not would I shed your memories as tears

instead all wear them as cape

fighting all the demons all the fears.

When you went away

some of me also went away

but as I continued to live

some of you also lived

"that some of you" from yesterday

constitutes all of me today.

Some people are gust of wind which clear away the clouds of despair .They are like wind which blows from place to place but never mistake wind for air they aren't supposed to linger but are meant to be remembered.

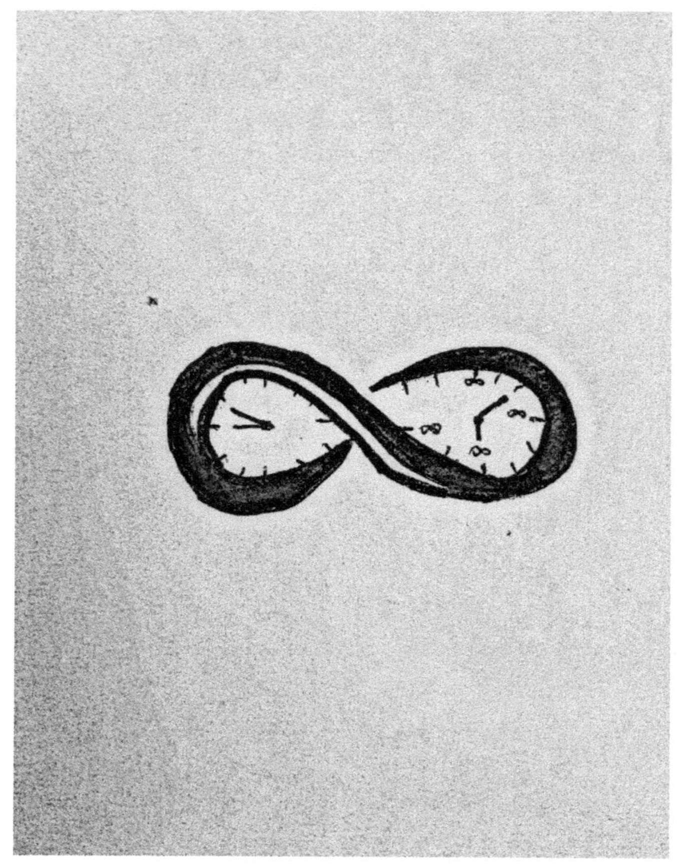

I know you are here

only my eyes can't see that you are here

but my heart knows so there's nothing to fear

there fore I won't shed any tear

I have seen you with my closed eyes

my anxious heart still calms down only to your lullabies

I have felt you without any physical form.

thanks to you in the frost I still feel warm

I try to be not sappy

I just pray you are happy

we are in a place far from words of longing

so rather than shouting out I miss you to the sky

I just whisper I love you to the wind

with the belief this wind can blow to the heavens.